Everything as Divine

The Wisdom of Meister Eckhart

Translated by
Edmund Colledge, O.S.A., and Bernard McGinn
Edited and with an introduction by
Stephen J. Connor

PAULIST PRESS
New York ◆ Mahwah, N.J.

Cover design by Tim McKeen. Cover photo by Don Kimball.

Library of Congress Cataloging-in-Publication Data

Eckhart, Meister, d. 1325.
    Everything as divine : the wisdom of Meister Eckhart / translated by Edmund Colledge and Bernard McGinn : edited and with an introduction by Stephen J. Connor.
        p.   cm.
    ISBN 0-8091-3675-9 (pbk.)
    1. Mysticism—Catholic Church. 2. Spiritual life—Catholic authors. 3. Catholic Church—Doctrines. I. Colledge, Edmund. II. McGinn, Bernard, 1937- . III. Connor, Stephen J. IV. Title.
    BV5080.E334 1996   96-13803
    248.4'82—dc20   CIP

Published by Paulist Press
997 Macarthur Boulevard
Mahwah, New Jersey 07430

Printed and bound in the
United States of America

CONTENTS

iv

INTRODUCTION

Many people today are hungering for the sacred in their lives. All we need to do is look at the best-seller lists to find titles which talk about spirituality and everyday life. In our Western Christian tradition, there are many great teachers and preachers who have given us insight into this search for the divine, the search for God in our lives. Meister Eckhart is one.

The speculation is that Eckhart was born around the year 1260. In this time period, birth records were not exact. Unless someone was in a noble family, there does not exist any exact recording of their birth. In Eckhart's case, this date is arrived at by future events in his life which can be dated. It is believed that he was born in the village of Hochheim, Germany, which is near Erfurt. This is determined by the fact that he entered the Dominican friars at Erfurt.

Eckhart's early years were spent in the usual education of the time in Latin grammar and the liberal arts. After this, he went for further studies to the monastery at Cologne where the Dominicans' institute was located. It is believed that he studied with Albert the Great. This would have brought Eckhart into contact with someone who had known and instructed Thomas Aquinas. This can be seen in Thomas' influence on Meister Eckhart's thought.

Eckhart's early life as a Dominican was spent preaching. Being known as the Order of Preachers, in their schools the Dominicans emphasized studying theology not as pure speculation but with the aim of preaching. In reading Eckhart's commentaries on sacred scripture, one can see the influence of preaching. Most writers of commentaries would present a whole exposition of an entire book of the scripture. Eckhart's commentaries take key passages and interpret them. This shows his concern and the Dominican influence on using theological studies within the discipline of preaching. These commentaries also demonstrate the wonderful way Eckhart himself used preaching as a way to convey his spiritual ideas.

Meister Eckhart spent many years training himself to be a theologian and philosopher. But he was also a great preacher and poet who loved to use wordplays, such as paradoxes, and unusual metaphors to keep his readers' intellectual and moral attention. This creative use of language is one of the reasons Eckhart's writing attracts people. However, it is precisely his playfulness with language which can make him difficult to understand. Though his use of language can be difficult, if readers persevere they are rewarded with a depth and understanding of prayer, mysticism and the workings of God in their lives. His understanding of detachment, the return of the soul to God and the birth of the Son of God in the soul continues to perplex his questioners and sustain his advocates. It is the depth of his message which makes him attractive to readers today.

In Part I of this book, we have taken excerpts from some of Eckhart's German sermons. As pointed out above, some of these excerpts show his wonderful use of wordplay to surprise the reader into a new way of thinking about God. For example, in the excerpt from Sermon 2, Eckhart uses the image of man as virgin. At first, this might seem a strange metaphor to use in illustrating one's relationship with God. For Eckhart, this image shows that there must not be "any obstacles between him and supreme truth, just as Jesus is empty and free and maidenly in himself."

Meister Eckhart understood the relationship between God and the human as intimate. He sees that our seeking of God does not lie in ways or programs or methods, but in detachment. We seek God through an awareness of the inward dwelling of the divine. God is beyond our ability to image the divine. In fact, to image God is to lose God and to embrace the image. We must go out of ourselves and "let God be God in you." He would say that even his own writing, his own wrestling with the divine workings in our world, must be abandoned because God is "a word unspoken." As his prayer states at the end of Sermon 5b: "That we may so truly remain within, that we may possess all truth, without medium and without distinction, in true blessedness, may God help us to do this. Amen."

One of Eckhart's most popular images is the birth of the Son of God in the soul. This is an image which permeates much of his writing. Eckhart believed that when we are free of all attachments we can open ourselves to receive the birth of the Son of God in our souls. This image of Eckhart's caused much controversy in his day. He believed that just "...as the Father in his simple nature gives his Son birth naturally, so truly does he give him birth in the inmost part of the spirit, and that is the inner world" (Sermon 5b). It is in this birth of God's Son in our soul that we find our ground, which is oneness with God.

In Part II of the book, we read from twenty-one different counsels that Eckhart delivered to young Dominicans during their evening meals. These particular counsels come under the general heading "On Discernment." Eckhart answers questions on diverse topics ranging from true obedience to what to do when God is hidden. Each of these counsels begins with a question or statement which is discussed by Eckhart. Each answer he gives contains important ideas and images from his thought and teaching. These responses to questions might be one of the best ways to grapple with Eckhart's ideas. As he answers these questions, one can see the workings of a great preacher and teacher. In this way, much of Eckhart's thoughts and beliefs are given in a manner that is more accessible to someone unfamiliar with his writings.

It is impossible to give a thorough understanding of Eckhart's thought in so small a volume. This book is an introduction to one of the great teachers and preachers of our Western spiritual tradition. Meister Eckhart gives us words and images which provoke us into deeper thought, into an articulation of the search of God in our lives. And yet, as Eckhart himself would probably agree, it is an articulation that is only a guide. Ultimately, we cannot hold on to the images; we need to let them go. We must open ourselves to listen, to see everything as divine, but not to make these images God. As humans, we communicate in language, in images. The same is true of how we come to understand the divine, the workings of God in our being and our world. But all images, all words fall short. They are only tools to help us detach and be open. I invite you to use these words, these images of Meister Eckhart to help point you towards the divine, towards God. But then, let them go. As Eckhart writes: "God is spoken and unspoken" (Sermon 53).

PART I

EXCERPTS FROM SELECTED SERMONS
(TRANSLATED FROM THE GERMAN)

SERMON 2

I have begun with a few words in Latin that are written in the gospel; and in German this means: "Our Lord Jesus Christ went up into a little town, and was received by a virgin who was a wife."

Now notice carefully what this says. It must necessarily be that the person by whom Jesus was received was a virgin. "Virgin" is as much as to say a person who is free of all alien images, as free as he was when he was not. Observe that people may ask how a man who has been born and has advanced to the age of reason could be as free of all images as when he was nothing; he who knows so many things that are all images: How then can he be free? Keep in mind this distinction, which I want to make clear for you. If I were so rational that there were present in my reason all the images that all men had ever received, and those that are present in God himself, and if I could be without possessiveness

7

in their regard, so that I had not seized possessively upon any one of them, not in what I did or what I left undone, not looking to past or to future, but I stood in this present moment free and empty according to God's dearest will, performing it without ceasing, then truly I should be a virgin, as truly unimpeded by any images as I was when I was not.

But I say that because a man is a virgin, that does not deprive him at all of any of the works he has ever done; but all this permits him to remain, maidenly and free, without any obstacles between him and supreme truth, just as Jesus is empty and free and maidenly in himself. As the authorities say that only between equals can unity be produced, so must a man be a maid and a virgin who is to receive the maidenly Jesus.

Now mark what I say and pay careful attention! For if a man were to be a virgin forever, no fruit would come from him. If he is to become fruitful, he must of necessity be a wife. "Wife" is the noblest word one can apply to the soul, much nobler than "virgin." That a man conceives God in himself is good, and in his conceiving he is a maiden. But that God should become fruitful in him is better; for the only gratitude for a gift is to be fruitful with the gift, and then the spirit is a wife, in its gratitude giving birth in return, when he for God gives birth again to Jesus into the heart of the Father.

And I have often said that there is a power in the soul that touches neither time nor flesh. It flows from the spirit and remains in the spirit and is wholly spiritual. In this power God is always verdant and blossoming in all the joy and the honor that he is in himself. That is a joy so heartfelt, a joy so incomprehensible and great that no one can tell it all. For it is in this power that the eternal Father ceaselessly brings his eternal Son so to birth, that this power also is bearing the Son of the Father, and bearing itself, that same Son, in the single power of the Father. If a man possessed a whole kingdom, or all the riches of the earth, and gave up the whole of it for the love of God and became one of the poorest men that ever lived on earth, and if God then gave him as much to suffer as he has ever given any man, and if he suffered it all until his death, and if God then gave him one single glimpse of what he is in this power, his joy would be so great that all this suffering and poverty would be too little. Yes, even if after this God never gave him the kingdom of heaven, he still would have received a reward great enough for all that

9

he had ever suffered, for God is present in this power as he is in the eternal now. If the spirit were always united with God in this power, the man could never grow old; for that now in which God made the first man, and the now in which the last man will have his end, and the now in which I am talking, they are all the same in God, and there is not more than the one now. Now you can see that this man lives in one light with God, and therefore there is not in him either suffering or the passage of time, but an unchanging eternity. From this man, truly, all wonderment has been taken away, and all things are essentially present in him. Therefore nothing new will come to him out of future events or accidents, for he dwells always anew in a now without ceasing. Such a divine lordship is there in this power.

SERMON 5B

That is what the text means with which I began: "God has sent his Only-Begotten Son into the world." You must not by this understand the external world in which the Son ate and drank with us, but understand it to apply to the inner world. As truly as the Father in his simple nature gives his Son birth naturally, so

10

truly does he give him birth in the most inward part of the spirit, and that is the inner world. Here God's ground is my ground, and my ground is God's ground. Here I live from what is my own, as God lives from what is his own. Whoever has looked for an instant into this ground, to such a man a thousand marks of red, minted gold are no more than a counterfeit penny. It is out of this inner ground that you should perform all your works without asking, "Why?" I say truly: So long as you perform your works for the sake of the kingdom of heaven, or for God's sake, or for the sake of your eternal blessedness, and you work them from without, you are going completely astray. You may well be tolerated, but it is not the best. Because truly, when people think that they are acquiring more of God in inwardness, in devotion, in sweetness and in various approaches than they do by the fireside or in the stable, you are acting just as if you took God and muffled his head up in a cloak and pushed him under a bench. Whoever is seeking God by ways is finding ways and losing God, who in ways is hidden. But whoever seeks for God without ways will find him as he is in himself, and that man will live with the Son, and he is life itself. If anyone went on for a thousand years asking of life: "Why are you living?" life, if it could only answer, would only say: "I live so that I may live." That is because life lives out of its own ground and springs from its own source, and so it lives without asking why it is itself living. If anyone asked a truthful man who works out of his own ground: "Why are you performing your works?" and if he were to give a straight answer, he would only say, "I work so that I may work."

Where the creature stops, there God begins to be. Now God wants no more from you than that you should in creaturely fashion go out of yourself, and let God be God in you. The smallest creaturely image that ever forms in you is as great as God is great. Why? Because it comes between you and the whole of God. As soon as the image comes in, God and all his divinity have to give way. But as the image goes out, God goes in. God wants you to go out of yourself in creaturely fashion as much as if all his blessedness consisted in it. O my dear man, what harm does it do you to allow God to be God in you? Go completely out of yourself for God's love, and God comes completely out of himself for love of you. And when these two have gone out, what remains there is a simplified One. In this One the

Father brings his Son to birth in the innermost source. Then the Holy Spirit blossoms forth, and then there springs up in God a will that belongs to the soul. So long as the will remains untouched by all created things and by all creation, it is free. Christ says: "No one comes into heaven except him who has come from heaven" (Jn 3:13). All things are created from nothing; therefore their true origin is nothing, and so far as this noble will inclines toward created things, it flows off with created things toward their nothing.

Now the question is: Does this noble will flow off in such a manner that it can never return? The authorities commonly say that it will never return, so far as it has flowed away in time. But I say: If this will turns away from itself and from all creation for one instant, and back to its first source, then the will stands in its true and free state, and it is free, and in this instant all lost time is restored.

People often say to me: "Pray for me." Then I think: Why are you coming out? Why do you not stay in yourself and hold on to your own good? After all, you are carrying all truth in you in an essential manner.

That we may so truly remain within, that we may possess all truth, without medium and without dis-

13

tinction, in true blessedness, may God help us to do this. Amen.

SERMON 22

"In the beginning." Here we are given to understand that we are an only son whom the Father has eternally borne out of the concealed darkness of the eternal concealment, remaining within in the first beginning of the first purity, which is a plentitude of all purity. Here I had my everlasting rest and sleep, in the eternal Father's hidden knowledge, remaining unspoken within. Out of the purity he everlastingly bore me, his only-born Son, into the same image of his eternal Fatherhood, that I may be Father and give birth to him of whom I am born. It is just as if someone were to stand before a high cliff and were to shout: "Are you there?" The echo of his voice would shout back: "Are you there?" If he were to say: "Come out of there!" the echo too would say: "Come out of there!" Yes, if someone saw a piece of wood in that light, it would become an angel and a rational being, and not merely rational; it would become pure reason in primal purity, for there is the plentitude of all purity. God acts like that: He gives birth to his Only-Begotten Son in the highest part of the soul. And as he gives birth to his Only-Begotten Son into me, so I give him birth again into the Father. That was not different from when God gave birth to the angel while he was born of the Virgin.

I wondered—this is many years ago—whether I would be asked how it is that each blade of grass can be so different from the others; and it happened that I was asked how they could be so different. I said: "What is more surprising is how they are all so alike." An authority said that the fact that all blades of grass are so different comes from the superabundance of God's goodness, which he pours superabundantly into all created things, so that his supremacy may be the more revealed. When I said: "It is more surprising that all the blades of grass are so alike," I went on, "just as all angels in the primal purity are all one angel, so are all blades of grass one in the primal purity, and all things there are one."

As I was coming here, I was thinking that in temporal existence man can reach the point where he is able to compel God. If I were up here, and I said to someone, "Come up here," that would be difficult. But if I were to say, "Sit down there," that would be easy. God acts like that. If a man humbles himself, God cannot withhold his own goodness but must come down and flow into the humble man, and to him who is least of all he gives himself the most of all, and he gives himself to him completely. What God gives is his being, and his being is his goodness, and his goodness is his love. All sorrow and all joy come from love. On the way, when I had to come here, I was thinking that I did not want to come here because I would become wet with tears of love. If you have ever been all wet with tears of love, let us leave that aside for now. Joy and sorrow come from love. A man ought not to fear God, for whoever fears him flees from him. This fear is a harmful fear. There is a rightful fear, when someone fears that he may lose God. A man should not fear him, he should love him, for God loves man with all his supreme perfection. The authorities say that all things work with the intention of giving birth and want to resemble the Father. They say: "The earth flees the heavens. If it flees downward, it comes down to the heavens; if it flees upward, it comes to the lowest part of the heavens." The earth can flee nowhere so deep that the heavens will not flow into it and impress their powers on it and make it fruitful, whether it likes this or not. This is how a man acts when he thinks that he can flee from God, and yet he cannot flee from him; every corner where he may go reveals God to him. He thinks that he is fleeing God, and he runs into his lap. God bears his Only-Begotten Son in you, whether you like it or not. Whether you are sleeping or waking, he does his part. Recently I asked whose fault it is if a man does not taste this, and I said that the fault was that his tongue was coated with some impurity, that is, with created things, just as with a man to whom all food is bitter and for whom nothing tastes good. Whose fault is it that food does not taste good to us? The fault is that we have no salt. The salt is divine love. If we had divine love, God would taste good to us, and all the works God every performed, and we should receive all things from God, and we should perform all the same works that he performs. In this likeness we are all one single Son.

When God created the soul, he created it according to his highest perfection, so that it might be a bride of the Only-Begotten Son. Because he knew this, he wanted to come forth from the secret treasure chamber of the eternal Fatherhood, in which he had eternally slept, unspoken, remaining within. "In the beginning." In the first beginning of the primal purity the Son had set up the pavilion of his everlasting glory, and he came out from there, from what was most exalted of all, because he wanted to exalt his beloved, whom the Father had eternally betrothed with him, so that he might bring her back again into the exaltation from which she came. Elsewhere it is written: "See! Your king is coming to you" (Zec 9:9). This is why he came out, and came leaping like a young hart (Sg 2:9), and suffered his torments for love, and he did not go out without wishing to go in again into his chamber with his bride. This chamber is the silent darkness of the hidden Fatherhood. When he went out from the highest place of all, he wanted to go in again with his bride to the purest place of all, and wanted to reveal to her the hidden secret of his hidden divinity, where he takes his rest with himself and with all created things.

In principio means in German as much as a beginning of all being, as I said in the school. I said more: It is an end of all being, for the first beginning is for the sake of the last end. Yes, God never takes rest there where he is the first beginning; he takes rest there where he is an end and a repose of all being, not that this being should

18

perish, but rather it is there perfected in its last end according to its highest perfection. What is the last end? It is the hidden darkness of the eternal divinity, and it is unknown, and it was never known, and it will never be known. God remains there within himself, unknown, and the light of the eternal Father has eternally shone in there, and the darkness does not comprehend the light (Jn 1:5). May the truth of which I have spoken help us that we may come to this truth. Amen.

SERMON 48

As I was coming here today I was wondering how I should preach to you so that it would make sense and you would understand it. Then I thought of a comparison: If you could understand that, you would understand my meaning and the basis of all my thinking in everything I have ever preached. The comparison concerns my eyes and a piece of wood. If my eye is open, it is an eye; if it is closed, it is the same eye. It is not the wood that comes and goes, but it is my vision of it. Now pay good heed to me! If it happens that my eye is in itself one and simple (Mt 6:22), and it is opened and casts its glance upon the piece of wood, the eye and the wood remain what they are, and yet in the act of vision they become as one, so that we can truly say that my eye is the wood and the wood is my eye. But if the wood were immaterial, purely spiritual as in the sight of my eye, then one could truly say that in the act of vision the wood and my eye subsisted in one being. If this is true of physical objects, it is far truer of spiritual objects.

You should know that my eye has far more in common with the eye of a sheep which is on the other side of the sea and which I never saw, than it has in common with my ears, with which, however, it shares its being; and that is because the action of the sheep's eye is also that of my eye. And so I attribute to both more in common in their action than I do to my eyes and my ears, because their actions are different.

Sometimes I have spoken of a light that is uncreated and not capable of creation and that is in the soul. I always mention this light in my sermons; and this same light comprehends God without a medium, uncovered, naked, as he is in himself; and this comprehension is to be understood as happening when the birth takes place. Here I may truly say that this light may have more unity with God than it has with any

power of the soul, with which, howe[...]
being. For you should know that this l[...]
in my soul's being than is the fee[...]
power, such as hearing or sight or an[...]
can be affected by hunger or thirst, [...]
the simplicity of my being is the cause o[...]
of this, if we take the powers as they are in our being,
they are all equally noble; but if we take them as they
work, one is much nobler and higher than another.

That is why I say that if a man will turn away from
himself and from all created things, by so much will
you be made one and blessed in the spark in the soul,
which has never touched either time or place. This
spark rejects all created things, and wants nothing but
its naked God, as he is in himself. It is not content with
the Father or the Son or the Holy Spirit, or with the
three Persons so far as each of them persists in his
properties. I say truly that his light is not content with
the divine nature's generative or fruitful qualities. I
will say more, surprising though this is. I speak in all
truth, truth that is eternal and enduring, that this same
light is not content with the simple divine essence in
its repose, as it neither gives nor receives; but it wants
to know the source of this essence, it wants to go into

e ground, into the quiet desert, into which ... ...ion never gazed, not the Father, nor the Son, ...he Holy Spirit. In the innermost part, where no ...e dwells, there is contentment for that light, and there it is more inward than it can be to itself, for this ground is a simple silence, in itself immovable, and by this immovability all things are moved, all life is received by those who in themselves have rational being.

May that enduring truth of which I have spoken help us that we may so have rational life. Amen.

SERMON 53

When I preach, I am accustomed to speak about detachment, and that a man should be free of himself and of all things; second, that a man should be formed again into that simple good which is God; third, that he should reflect on the great nobility with which God has endowed his soul, so that in this way he may come to wonder at God; fourth, about the purity of the divine nature, for the brightness of the divine nature is beyond words. God is a word, a word unspoken.

Augustine says: "All writings are in vain. If one says that God is a word, he has been expressed; but if one says that God has not been spoken, he is ineffable." And yet he is something, but who can speak this word? No one can do this, except him who is this Word. God is a Word that speaks itself. Wherever God is, he speaks this Word; wherever he is not, he does not speak. God is spoken and unspoken. The Father is a speaking work, and the Son is speech working. Whatever is in me proceeds from me; if I only think it, my word manifests it, and still it remains in me. So does the Father speak the unspoken Son, and yet the Son remains in him. And I have often said: "God's going out is his going in." To the extent that I am close to God, so to that extent God utters himself into me. The more that all rational creatures in their works go out of themselves, the more they go into themselves. This is not so with merely corporeal creatures; the more they work, the more they go out of themselves. All creatures want to utter God in all their works; they all come as close as they can in uttering him, and yet they cannot utter him. Whether they wish it or not, whether they like it or not, they all want to utter God, and yet he remains unuttered.

PART II:
SELECTIONS FROM THE COUNSELS ON DISCERNMENT

*T*hese are the conversations that the vicar of Thuringia, the prior of Erfurt, Friar Eckhart of the Order of Preachers, held with those young men who, conversing, asked him about many things as they sat with each other at the evening meal.

Counsel 1. *First, about true obedience.*

True and perfect obedience is a virtue above all virtues, and no work is so great that it can be achieved or done without this virtue; and however little and however humble a work may be, it is done to greater profit in true obedience, be it saying Mass, hearing it, praying, contemplating or whatever else you can think of. But take as humble a work as you like, whatever it may be, true obedience makes it finer and better for you. Obedience always produces the best of everything in everything. Truly, obedience never perturbs, never fails, whatever one is doing, in anything that comes from true obedience, for obedience neglects

24

nothing that is good. Obedience need never be troubled, for it lacks no good thing.

When a man in obedience goes out of himself and renounces what he possesses, God must necessarily respond by going in there, for if anyone does not want something for himself, God must want it as if for himself. If I deny my own will, putting it in the hands of my superior, and want nothing for myself, then God must want it for me, and if he fails me in this matter, he will be failing himself. So in all things, when I do not want something for myself, God wants it for me. Now pay good heed. What is it that God wants for me that I do not want for myself? When I empty myself of self, he must necessarily want everything for me that he wants for himself. And if he were not to do this, by that truth which is God, he would not be just, nor would he be the God that it is his nature to be.

In true obedience there should be no trace of "I want it so, or so," or "I want this or that," but there should be a pure going out from what is yours. And therefore in the best of all prayers that a man can pray, there should not be "Give me this virtue, or that way of life," or "Yes, Lord, give me yourself, or give me everlasting life," but "Lord, give me nothing but what you will, and do,

Lord, whatever and however you will in every way." That is superior to the first way of praying as the heavens are above the earth. And when one has concluded that prayer, one has prayed well, for then one has in true obedience wholly entered into God. And just as true obedience should have no "I want it so," so also one should not hear from obedience "I do not want," because "I do not want" is a sure poison of all obedience. That is what Saint Augustine says: "God's faithful servant has no desire for people to say or to give to him, or what he likes to hear or see, for his first and his greatest aim is to hear what is most pleasing to God."

Counsel 2. *Of the most powerful prayer, and of the highest work of all.*

The most powerful prayer, and almost the strongest of all to obtain everything, and the most honorable of all works, is that which proceeds from an empty spirit. The emptier the spirit, the more is the prayer and the work mighty, worthy, profitable, praiseworthy and perfect. The empty spirit can do everything.

What is an empty spirit?

An empty spirit is one that is confused by nothing, attached to nothing, has not attached its best to any

26

fixed way of acting, and has no concern whatever in anything for its own gain, for it is all sunk deep down into God's dearest will and has forsaken its own. A man can never perform any work, however humble, without it gaining strength and power from this.

We ought to pray so powerfully that we should like to put our every member and strength, our two eyes and ears, mouth, heart and all our senses to work; and we should not give up until we find that we wish to be one with him who is present to us and whom we entreat, namely God.

Counsel 3. Of people who have not denied themselves and are full of their own will.

People say: "O Lord, how much I wish that I stood as well with God, that I had as much devotion and peace in God as others have, I wish that it were so with me!" Or, "I should like to be poor," or else, "Things will never go right for me till I am in this place or that, or till I act one way or another. I must go and live in a strange land, or in a hermitage, or in a cloister."

In fact, this is all about yourself, and nothing else at all. This is just self-will, only you do not know it or it does not seem so to you. There is never any trouble that starts in you that does not come from your own will, whether people see this or not. We can think what we like, that a man ought to shun one thing or pursue another—places and people and ways of life and environments and undertakings—that is not the trouble, such ways of life or such matters are not what impedes you. It is what you are in these things that causes the trouble, because in them you do not govern yourself as you should.

Therefore, make a start with yourself, and abandon yourself. Truly, if you do not begin by getting away from yourself, wherever you run to, you will find obstacles and trouble wherever it may be. People who seek peace in external things—be it in places or ways of life or people or activities or solitude or poverty or degradation—however great such a thing may be or whatever it may be, still it is all nothing and gives no peace. People who seek in that way are doing it all wrong; the further they wander, the less will they find what they are seeking. They go around like someone who has lost his way; the further he goes, the more lost he is. Then what ought he to do? He ought to begin by forsaking himself, because then he has forsaken everything. Truly, if a man renounced a kingdom or the whole world but held on to himself, he would not have renounced anything. What is more, if a man renounces himself, whatever else he retains, riches or honors or whatever it may be, he has forsaken everything.

About what Saint Peter said: "See, Lord, we have forsaken everything" (Mt 19:27)—and all that he had forsaken was just a net and his little boat—there is a saint who says: "If anyone willingly gives up something little, that is not all which he has given up, but he has forsaken everything which worldly men can gain and what they can even long for; for whoever has renounced his own will and himself has renounced everything, as truly as if he had possessed it as his own, to dispose of as he would." For what you choose not to long for, you have wholly forsaken and renounced for the love of God. That is why our Lord said: "Blessed are the poor in spirit" (Mt 5:3), that is, in the will. And no one ought to be in doubt about this; if there were a better form of living, our Lord would have said so, as he also said: "Whoever wishes to come after me, let him deny himself" (Mt 16:24), as a beginning; everything depends on that. Take a look at yourself, and whenever you find yourself, deny yourself. That is the best of all.

29

Counsel 4. *Of the profits of self-abandonment, which*
one should practice inwardly and outwardly.

You should know that there was never any man in
this life who forsook himself so much that he could not
still find more in himself to forsake. There are few people who see this to be true and stick by it. This is indeed
a fair exchange and an honest deal: By as much as you
go out in forsaking all things, by so much, neither less
nor more, does God go in, with all that is his, as you
entirely forsake everything that is yours. Undertake
this, and let it cost you everything you can afford.
There you will find true peace, and nowhere else.

People ought never to think too much about what
they could do, but they ought to think about what
they could be. If people and their way of life were only
good, what they did might be a shining example. If
you are just, then your works too are just. We ought
not to think of building holiness upon action; we
ought to build it upon a way of being, for it is not
what we do that makes us holy, but we ought to make
holy what we do. However holy the works may be,
they do not, as works, make us at all holy; but, as we
are holy and have being, to that extent we make all our
works holy, be it eating, sleeping, keeping vigil or

whatever it may be. It does not matter what men may do whose being is mean; nothing will come of it. Take good heed: We ought to do everything we can to be good; it does not matter so much what we may do, or what kinds of works ours may be. What matters is the ground on which the works are built.

Counsel 5. *See what can make our being and our ground good.*

A man's being and ground—from which his works derive their goodness—is good when his intention is wholly directed to God. Set all your care on that, that God become great within you, and that all your zeal and effort in everything you do and in everything you renounce be directed toward God. Truly, the more you do this in all your works, whatever they are, the better they are. Cleave to God, and he will endow you with all goodness. Seek God, and you will find God and every good thing as well. Yes, truly, with such an attitude you could tread upon a stone, and that would be a more godly thing for you to do than for you to receive the Body of our Lord, if then you were thinking more of yourself with less detachment. If we cling to God, then God and all virtues cling to us. And what once you were seeking now seeks you; what once you hunted after now hunts you, and what you once wished to shun now avoids you. Therefore to him who clings greatly to God, everything clings that is godly, and from him everything takes flight that is unlike God and alien to him.

Counsel 6. Of detachment and of the possession of God.

I was asked: "Since some people keep themselves much apart from others, and most of all like to be alone, and since it is in this and in being in church that they find peace, would that be the best thing to do?" Then I said: "No! and see why not!" If all is well with a man, then truly, wherever he may be, whomever he may be with, it is well with him. But if things are not right with him, then everywhere and with everybody it is all wrong with him. If it is well with him, truly he has God, he has him everywhere, in the street and in company with everyone, just as much as in church or in solitary places or in his cell. But if a man really has God, and has only God, then no one can hinder him.

Why?

Because he has only God, and his intention is toward God alone, and all things become for him nothing but God. That man carries God in his every work and in every place, and it is God alone who performs all the man's works; for whoever causes the work, to him it belongs more properly and truly than it does to the one who performs it. Then let our intention be purely and only for God, and then truly he must perform all our works, and no person, no crowds, no places can hinder him in all his works. In the same way, no one can hinder this man, for he intends and seeks and takes delight in nothing but God, for God has become one with the man in all his intention. And so, just as no multiplicity can disturb God, nothing can disturb or fragment this man, for he is one in that One where all multiplicity is one and is one unmultiplicity.

A man should accept God in all things, and should accustom himself to having God present always in his disposition and his intention and his love. Take heed how you can have God as the object of your thoughts whether you are in church or in your cell. Preserve and carry with you that same disposition when you are in crowds and in uproar and in unlikeness. And, as I have said before, when one speaks of likeness, one does not mean that we should pay like attention to all works or all places or all people. That would be quite wrong, because praying is a better work than spinning, and the church is a better place than the street. But you ought in your works to have a like disposition and a like confidence and a like love for your God and a like seriousness. Believe me, if you were constant in this way, no one could become between you and the God who is present to you.

But a man in whom truly God is not but who must grasp God in this thing or in that from outside, and who seeks God in unlike ways, be it in works or people or places, such a man does not possess God. And it may easily be that something hinders such a man for he does not possess God, and he does not seek him alone, nor does he love and intend him alone; and therefore it is not only bad company that hinders him. Good company can also hinder him—not just the street, but the church too, not only evil words and deeds, but good words and deeds as well, for the hindrance is in him, because in him God has not become all things. Were that so, everything would be right and good for him, in every place and among all people, because he has God, and no one can take God away from him or hinder him in his work.

On what does this true possession of God depend, so that we may truly have him?

This true possession of God depends on the disposition, and on an inward directing of the reason and intention toward God, not on a constant contemplation in an unchanging manner, for it would be impossible to nature to preserve such an intention, and very laborious, and not the best thing either. A man ought not to have a God who is just a product of his thought, nor should he be satisfied with that, because if the thought vanished, God too would vanish. But one ought to have a God who is present, a God who is far above the notions of men and of all created things. That God does not vanish, if a man does not willfully turn away from him.

The man who has God essentially present to him grasps God divinely, and to him God shines in all things; for everything tastes to him of God, and God forms himself for the man out of all things. God always shines out in him, in him there is a detachment and a turning away, and a forming of his God whom he loves and who is present to him. It is like a man consumed with a real and burning thirst, who may well not drink and may turn his mind to other things. But whatever he may do, in whatever company he may be, whatever he may be intending or thinking of or working at, still the idea of drinking does not leave him, so long as he is thirsty. The more his thirst grows, the more the idea of drinking grows and intrudes and possesses him and will not leave him. Or if a man loves something ardently and with all his heart, so that nothing else has savor for him or touches his heart but that, and that and nothing but that is his whole object: Truly, wherever he is, whomever he is with, whatever he may undertake, whatever he does, what he so loves never passes from his mind, and he finds the image of what he loves in everything, and it is the more present to him the more his love grows and grows. He does not seek rest, because no unrest hinders him.

Such a man finds far greater merit with God because he grasps everything as divine and as greater than things in themselves are. Truly, to this belong zeal and love and a clear apprehension of his own inwardness, and a lively, true, prudent and real knowledge of what his disposition is concerned with amid things and persons. A man cannot learn this by running away, by shunning things and shutting himself up in an external solitude; but he must practice a solitude of the spirit, wherever or with whomever he is. He must learn to break through things and to grasp his God in them and to form him in himself powerfully in an essential manner. This is like someone who wants to learn to write. If he is to acquire the art, he must certainly practice it hard and long, however disagreeable and difficult this may be for him and however impossible it may seem. If he will practice it industriously and assiduously, he learns it and masters the art. To begin with, he must indeed memorize each single letter and get it firmly into his mind. Then, when he has the art, he will not need to think about and remember the letters' appearance; he can write effortlessly and easily—and it will be the same if he wants to play the fiddle or to learn any other skill. It will always be enough for him to make up his mind to do the hard work the art demands; and even if he is not thinking about it all the time, still, whatever he may be thinking when he does perform it, this will be from the art he has learned.

So a man must be penetrated with the divine presence, and be shaped through and through with the shape of the God he loves, and be present in him, so that God's presence may shine out to him without any effort. What is more, in all things let him acquire nakedness, and let him always remain free of things. But at the beginning there must be attentiveness and a careful formation within himself, like a schoolboy setting himself to learn.

Counsel 7. *How a man should perform his work in the most reasonable way.*

One often finds people who are not impeded by the things that are around them—and this is easy to attain if one wishes—nor do they have any constant thought about them. For if the heart is full of God, created things can have and find no place in it. But, what is more, this alone should not satisfy us. We ought to turn everything into great profit, whatever it may be, wherever we may be, whatever we see or hear, however strange or unlikely it may be. Then for the first time all is well with us and not until then, and one will never come to an end in this. One can always go on increasing in this, gaining more and more from it in true growth.

And in all his activities and under all circumstances a man should take care to use his reason, and in everything he should have a reasonable consciousness of himself and of his inwardness, and find God in all things, in the highest degree that is possible. For a man ought to be as our Lord said: "You should be like men who are always watching and waiting for their master"

(Lk 12:36). Truly, people who wait stay awake and look around them for whence he for whom they are waiting may be coming; and they are on the lookout for him in whatever may come, however unknown it may be to them, for perhaps he might somehow be in it. So we should have in all things a knowing perception of our master. We must show zeal in this, and it must cost us everything we are capable of in mind and body, and so it will be well with us, and we shall find God in everything alike, and find God always alike in all things.

Certainly, one work differs from another; but whoever undertakes all his works in the same frame of mind, then, truly, all that man's works are the same. Indeed, for the man for whom God shines forth as directly in worldly things as he does in divine things and to whom God would be so present, for such a man things would be well. Not indeed that the man himself would be doing worldly things, unlike to God; rather, whatever external matters he chanced to see and hear, he would refer it all back to God. Only he to whom God is present in everything and who employs his reason in the highest degree and has enjoyment in it knows anything of true peace and has a real kingdom of heaven.

For if things are to go well with a man, one of two things must always happen to him. Either he must find and learn to possess God in works, or he must abandon all works. But since a man cannot in this life be without works, which are proper to humans and are of so many kinds, therefore he must learn to possess his God in all things and to remain unimpeded, whatever he may be doing, wherever he may be. And therefore if a man who is beginning must do something with other people, he ought first to make a powerful petition to God for his help, and put him immovably in his heart and unite all his intentions, thoughts, will and power to God, so that nothing else than God can take shape in that man.

Counsel 8. *Of constant zeal for the highest growth.*

A man should never be so satisfied with what he does or accomplish it in such a way that he becomes so independent or overconfident in his works that his reason becomes idle or lulled to sleep. He ought always to lift himself up by the two powers of reason and will, and in this to grasp at what is best of all for him in the highest degree, and outwardly and inwardly to guard prudently against everything that could harm him. So in all things he will lack nothing, but he will grow constantly and mightily.

Counsel 9. How the inclination to sin
always helps a man.

You must know that when vices attack us, this is never for the just man without great profit and utility. See carefully. There are two men, and one of them may be so disposed that shortcomings never or seldom touch him; but it is the other man's nature that they do. The outward presence of things so stirs the outer man in him that he is easily moved to anger or to vain ambition or it may be to bodily lusts, whatever the circumstance may be. But in his highest powers he always stands firm and unmoved, never willing to commit sin, because the sin is perhaps a weakness of his nature, as many men are naturally wrathful or proud or whatever it may be, and yet he does not want to sin. This man is far more to be praised, and his reward is much greater and his virtue is much more excellent than that of the first man, for the perfection of virtue comes from fighting, as Saint Paul says: "Virtue is made perfect in infirmity" (2 Cor 12:9).

The inclination to sin is not sin, but to want to sin

is sin, to want to be angry is sin. Indeed, if a man thought rightly, and if he had the power to choose, he would not want to choose that his inclination to sin should die in him, because without it he would lack decision in everything and in all that he did he would be without care in these matters, and, too, he would lose the honor of the battle and of the victory and of the reward; for it is the assault and the force of vice that bring virtue and the reward for striving. It is this inclination that makes a man ever more zealous to exercise himself valiantly in virtue and impels him mightily toward virtue, and it is a stern whip driving a man on to caution and virtue. For the weaker a man finds himself, the more should he protect himself with strength and victory. For virtue and vice too are a question of the will.

Counsel 10. *How the will can do all things, and how all virtues are a question of the will, if only it is just.*

A man should not be too afraid of anything, so long as he sees that he has good will, nor should he be depressed if he cannot accomplish his will in his deeds; but he should not consider himself deprived of virtue if he finds in himself a will that is just and good, because the virtues and everything that is good are a question of good will. You can want for nothing if you have a true and just will, not love or humility or any virtue. But what you desire with all your might and all your will, that you have, and God and all created things cannot take it away from you, if only your will is wholly just and godly and is directed toward the present. So do not say: "One day I should like...," because that would be for the future, but "I want it to be so now." Pay good attention: If something is more than a thousand miles away and I want to have it, I really have it—more than what is lying in my lap and what I do not want.

What is good has not less power to draw toward good than what is evil has to draw toward evil. Pay heed: Though I might never perform any evil deed, if I have the will to evil, I have the sin, as if I had performed the deeds; and I could commit as great sins only in my will as if I had murdered the whole human race, even if I had actually never done anything of the kind. So why should the same thing not be true of a good will? Truly, and far more so!

Indeed, with my will I can do everything. I can take on myself every man's toil, I can feed every poor man, I can do every man's work and anything else that you could think of. If you are not lacking in will but only in power, in truth in God's sight you have done it all, and no one can take it away from you, or stop you for a moment from doing it; for wanting to do something as soon as I can and having done it are the same in the sight of God. What is more, if I wanted to have as great a will as the whole world has, and if my longing for that is great and complete, then indeed I have it; for what I want to have, I have. And, too, if I truly wanted to have as much love as all men have ever gained, or to praise God as much, or anything else you can think of, then indeed, you have it all, if only your will is complete.

Now you might ask, "When is the will a just will?"

The will is complete and just when it is without any self-seeking, and when it has forsaken itself, and has been formed and shaped into God's will. And the more this is so with a man, the more is his will just and true. And in that will you can accomplish everything, be it love or whatever you want.

Now you ask: "How could I have this love, whilst I do not feel it and am not aware of it, and yet I see many people who accomplish great deeds, and I see in them great devotion and marvelous qualities I do not have?"

44

Here you ought to observe two properties that love possesses; one is the being of love, the other is the deeds or the manifestation of love. The place where love has its being is only in the will; the man who has more will, he also has more love. But no one knows about anyone else, whether he has more of it; that lies hidden in the soul, so long as God lies hidden in the soul's ground. This love lies wholly in the will; whoever has more will, he also has more love.

Yet there is something else, which is a manifestation and a deed of love. Often this appears plainly as inwardness and devotion and jubilation; and yet this is not always the best that could be. For it may be that it does not come from love, but perhaps it only comes from nature that a man experiences such savor and sweetness. It may be sent down from heaven, or it may be borne in from the senses. And those who have more of this are not always the best men; for even if such a gift be truly from God, our Lord often gives it to such people to entice and draw them on, and also to make them, through it, very withdrawn from others. Yet these same people, when later they have obtained more love, may then well not experience so much emotion and feeling, and from that it is well seen that they have love, if they cleave faithfully and steadily to God without such a prop.

And even if this really be love, it still is not the very best love. That can be seen when sometimes a man must abandon this kind of jubilation because of a better kind of love, and sometimes to perform a work of love, whether spiritual or bodily, when someone has need of him. I have said before: If a man were in an ecstasy, as Saint Paul was, and knew that some sick man needed him to give him a bit of soup, I should think it far better if you would abandon your ecstasy out of love and show greater love in caring for the other in his need.

Nor should a man think that in doing so he will be deprived of grace, for whatever he willingly abandons out of love will become a much greater reward for him, as Christ said: "Whoever has given up something for love of me, he will receive in return a hundred times as much" (Mt 19:29). Yes, truly, when a man forsakes something and denies it to himself for the love of God, yes, even if it be that a man has a great desire to experience such consolations and inwardness and does everything he can to obtain this and God does not give it to him, and he willingly relinquishes and forgoes

46

this for God's love, then such a man will find in God what he seeks, just as if he had possessed as his own all the riches that ever were and had willingly relinquished, abandoned and denied them for God's sake. He will receive a hundred times as much. For whatever a man would gladly have that he relinquishes and goes without for God's love, be it something material or spiritual, he will find all of it in God, just as if he had possessed it and had willingly abandoned it; for a man ought gladly be robbed of all that he has for the love of God, and out of love he should wholly abandon and deny love's consolations.

That a man ought sometimes out of love to forgo such sensations, Saint Paul in his love admonishes us when he says: "I have wished that I might be separated from Christ for the love of my brothers" (Rom 9:3). By that he means not the pure love of God, for from that he did not wish to be separated for one instant, nor for the sake of everything that might be in heaven and on earth. He means the consolation of love.

But you must know that God's friends are never without consolation, for whatever God wills is for them the greatest consolation of all, whether it be consolation or desolation.

Counsel 11. What a man should do when God has hidden himself and he seeks for him in vain.

You ought also to know that a man with good will can never lose God. Rather, it sometimes seems to his feelings that he loses him, and often he thinks that God has gone far away. What ought you to do then? Just what you did when you felt the greatest consolation; learn to do the same when you are in the greatest sorrow, and under all circumstances behave as you did then. There is no advice so good as to find God where one has left him; so do now, when you cannot find him, as you were doing when you had him; and in that way you will find him. But a good will never loses or seeks in vain for God. Many people say: "We have a good will," but they do not have God's will. They want to have their will and they want to teach our Lord that he should be doing this and that. That is not a good will. We ought to seek from God what is his very dearest will.

This is what God looks for in all things, that we surrender our will. When Saint Paul had done a lot of talking to our Lord, and our Lord had reasoned much with him, that produced nothing, until he surrendered his will, and said: "Lord, what do you want me to do?"

(Acts 9:6). Then our Lord showed him clearly what he ought to do. So too, when the angel appeared to our Lady, nothing either she or he had to say would ever have made her the Mother of God, but as soon as she gave up her own will, at that moment she became a true mother of the everlasting Word and she conceived God immediately; he became her Son by nature. Nor can anything make a true man except giving up his will. Truly, without giving up our own will in all things, we never accomplish anything in God's sight. But if it were to progress so far that we gave up the whole of our will and had the courage to renounce everything, external and internal, for the love of God, then we would have accomplished all things, and not until then.

We find few people, whether they know it or not, who would not like this to be so for them: to experience great things, to have this way of living and this treasure. But all this is nothing in them except self-will. You ought to surrender yourself wholly to God in all things, and then do not trouble yourself about what he may do with his own. There are thousands of people, dead and in heaven, who never truly and perfectly forsook their own wills. Only a perfect and true will could make one enter perfectly into God's will and be without will of one's own; and whoever has more of this, he is more fully and more truly established in God. Yes, one Hail Mary said when a man has abandoned himself is more profitable than to read the Psalms a thousand times over without that. With that, one pace forward would be better than to walk across the sea without it.

The man who in this way had wholly gone out of himself with everything that he possessed would indeed be established wholly in God, so that if anyone wanted to move him, he would first have to move God. For he is wholly in God, and God is around him as my cap is round my head. If anyone wanted to seize hold of me, first he would have to seize hold of my coat. In the same way, if I want to drink, the drink must first pass over my tongue; in this way the drink gives its flavor. If the tongue is coated with bitterness, then truly, however sweet the wine itself may be, it must become bitter through the means by which it comes to me. In truth, if a man had completely abandoned everything that is his, he would be so surrounded by God that no created thing could move him, unless it had first moved God. Whatever would reach him would first have to reach him by means of God. So it will find its savor from God, and will become godlike. However great a sorrow may be, if it comes by means of God, then God has suffered it first. Yes, by that Truth which is God, however little a sorrow may be that comes upon a man, as he places it in God, be it some displeasure or contradiction, it moves God immeasurably more than the man, and if it is grievous for the man it is more so for God. But God suffers it for the sake of some good thing that he has provided in it for you, and if you will suffer the sorrow that God suffers and that comes to you through him, it will easily become godlike—contempt, it may be, just as respect; bitterness just as sweetness; the greatest darkness just as the brightest light. It takes all its savor from God, and it becomes godlike, for it forms itself wholly in his image, whatever comes to this man, for this is all his intention and nothing else has savor for him; and in this he accepts God in all bitterness, just as in the greatest sweetness.

The light shines in darkness, and there man perceives it. What is the use to people of teaching or light, unless they use it? If they are in darkness or sorrow, they ought to see the light.

Yes, the more that we possess ourselves, the less do we possess. The man who has gone out of what is his own could never fail to find God in anything he did.

But if it happened that a man did or said something amiss, or engaged in matters that were wrong, then God, since he was in the undertaking at the beginning, must of necessity take this harm upon him too; but you must under no circumstances abandon your undertaking because of this. We find an example of this in Saint Bernard and in many other saints. One can never in this life be wholly free from such mishaps. But because some weeds happen among the corn, one should not for that reason throw away the good corn. Indeed, if it were well with a man and he knew himself well with God, all such sorrows and mishaps would turn into his great profit. For to good men all things come to good, as Saint Paul says (Rom 8:28).; and, as Saint Augustine says, "Yes, even sins."

Counsel 12. Of sins and of how we should act when we find ourselves in sin.

Indeed, to have committed sins is not sin, if we have sorrow for them. A man should never wish to commit sin, not for anything that could be in time or in eternity, not mortal sins, not venial, not any sins at all. A man who knew himself well with God ought always to see that our faithful and loving God has brought man out of a sinful life into a life that is divine, and out of him who was his enemy God has made a friend, and that is more than to create a new earth. This would be one of the greatest reasons for a man to become wholly established in God; and it would be astonishing how greatly it would kindle the man to a stronger and greater love, so that he would wholly abandon what is his own.

Yes, that man would indeed be established in God's will who would not wish that the sin into which he had fallen had never been committed; not because it was against God, but since, through that, you are obliged to greater love, and through that, brought low and humbled. He should only wish that he had not acted against God. But you should indeed trust God, that he would not have inflicted this on you, had he not wished to produce from it what is best for you. But when a man with all his resolution rises up from his sins and turns wholly away from them, our faithful God then acts as if he had never fallen into sin. For all his sins, God will not allow him for one moment to suffer. Were they as many as all men have ever committed, God will never allow him to suffer for this. With this man God can use all of the simple tenderness that he has ever shown toward created beings. If he now finds the man ready to be different, he will have no regard for what he used to be. God is a God of the present. He takes and receives you as he finds you—not what you have been, but what you are now. All the harms and the insults that could come upon God for all sins he is gladly willing to suffer and to have suffered for many years so that a man thereafter may come to a greater knowledge of his love and so that man's love and gratitude may be so much greater and his zeal may be so much more ardent, which properly and frequently follows after our sins.

Therefore God gladly suffers the harm of sins, and has often suffered it, and most often he has permitted it to happen to men for whom he has provided that he would draw them to great things. Notice well: Who was dearer or closer to our Lord than were the apostles? But there was no one of them who did not fall into mortal sin; they had all been mortal sinners. In the Old Law and the New he often showed this through men who afterward were by far the dearest to him. And even now one seldom finds that people attain to anything good unless first they have gone somewhat astray. Our Lord's intention in this is that we should recognize his great mercifulness; and through it he wishes to exhort us to a greater and truer humility and devotion. For when repentance is renewed, so too love should be greatly increased and renewed.

Counsel 13. *Of a twofold repentance.*

Repentance is of two kinds; one is of time and of the senses, the other is divine and supernatural. Repentance in time always declines into greater sorrow and plunges a man into lamentation, as if he must now despair; and there repentance remains in its sorrow, and can make no progress; nothing comes of it.

But divine repentance is quite different. As soon as a man has achieved self-loathing, at once he lifts himself up to God, and establishes himself in an eternal turning away from all sin in an immovable will; and there he lifts himself up in great confidence to God, and achieves a great security. And from this there comes a spiritual joy that lifts the soul up out of all sorrow and lamentation, and makes it secure in God. For the weaker a man finds himself and the more have been his misdeeds, the more cause he has to bind himself to God with an undivided love in which there is no sin or weakness. Therefore the best path up which a man can proceed when he wants to go to God in all devotion, is for him to be sinless, made strong by a godly repentance.

And the heavier a man's sins are as he weighs them, the readier is God to forgive them, and to come to the soul, and to drive the sins out. Every man does his utmost to get rid of what most irks him. And the greater and the more the sins are, still immeasurably more is God glad and ready to forgive them, because they are irksome to him. And then, as godly repentance lifts itself up to God, sins vanish into God's abyss, faster than it takes me to shut my eyes, and so they become utterly nothing, as if they had never happened, if repentance is complete.

Counsel 14. Of true confidence and of hope.

One ought to test whether love be true and perfect by asking if one has great hope and confidence in God, for there is nothing by which one can better see whether one's love is total than by trust. For if one man loves another greatly and completely, that causes him to have trust; for everything that we dare trust to be in God we find in him truly and a thousand times more. And so, since no man could ever love God too much, so also no man could ever trust him too much. Nothing that a man can do is so fitting as to have great trust in God. God never ceased to achieve great things through those who ever gained great confidence in him. He has truly shown to all men that this trusting comes from love, for love not only has trust, it also has true knowledge and unshakeable certainty.

Counsel 15. Of a twofold certainty of everlasting life.

In this life we have a twofold knowledge of everlasting life. One knowledge is when God himself imparts it to a man or sends it to him through an angel or shows it through a special illumination; this happens seldom and to few people.

The second knowledge, which is incomparably better and more profitable and happens often to all who are perfect in their love, is when a man, through the love and the intimacy that exist between his God and him, trusts in him so fully and is so certain of him that he cannot doubt. What makes him so certain is that he loves God in all his creatures without any distinction. And even if all God's creatures were to deny him and abjure him, yes, if God himself were to deny him, he would not mistrust; for love cannot mistrust,

love has trust in everything that is good. There is n[o]
need for one to say anything to the lover and to hi[s]
beloved, for once the lover knows that his belove[d]
loves him, he knows at once everything that is for hi[s]
good and makes for his happiness. For however grea[t]
your love for him may be, of this you are sure: His lov[e]
for you is greater beyond measure, and his trust in yo[u]
is incomparably more. For he is Trust himself; on[e]
should be sure of this with him, and they are all sur[e]
of it who love him.

This certainty is by far greater, more complete an[d]
true than is the first, and it cannot deceive. To be tol[d]
it in words could deceive, and could easily be a fals[e]
light. But this certainty one receives in all the power[s]
of the soul, and it cannot deceive those who truly lov[e]
God; they doubt as little as a man doubts in God
because love drives out all fear. "Love has no fear," a[s]
Saint Paul says, and as it is also written: "Love covers [a]
multitude of sins" (1 Pt 4:8). For when sins occur
there cannot be complete trust or love, for love com[-]
pletely covers sin over; love knows nothing about sin[.]
It is not as if a man had not sinned, but that love whol[-]
ly destroys and drives out sin, as if it had never been[.]
For all God's works are wholly perfect and superabun[-]

dant, so that whomever he forgives, he forgives wholly
and completely, and great sinners more gladly than
the lesser ones, and this makes a perfect trust. I esti-
mate this to be far and incomparably better than the
first knowledge; and it brings a greater reward and is
more true, for it is not hindered by sin or by anything
else. For if God finds a man to be in such a state of
love, he judges him just as lovingly, whether or not the
man may have done something greatly amiss. But the
man who receives greater forgiveness should love
more, as Christ our Lord said: "To whom more is forgiven, let him love more" (Lk 7:47).

Counsel 16. Of true penitence and a blessed life.

Many people think that they ought to perform great
exterior works, such as fasting, going barefoot and
such things as that, which are called "penitence." But
the true and very best of all penitence, which greatly
improves men and raises them to the highest, is for a
man to have a great and perfect aversion from everything in himself and in all creatures that is not wholly
God and godly, and for him to have a great and perfect
and complete conversion to his dear God in a love so
unshakeable that his devotion to God and his longing

for him be great. The more you have of this in any work, the more you are justified; and as this grows and grows, so you have more and more true penitence, and this will the more blot out sin and even sin's punishment. Yes, you could in a short time with great resolution turn away from all sin with a true disgust for it, and with equal resolution betake yourself to God, so that even if you had committed all the sins that have ever been done since the days of Adam and will ever be done, all that would be completely forgiven you and its punishment remitted, so that if you were to die this moment you would come into the presence of God.

This is true penitence, and it comes, particularly and most perfectly, from what our Lord Jesus Christ suffered so fruitfully in his perfect penitence. The more that a man forms himself in that, the more do all sins and the pains of sin fall away from him. And it ought to be a man's habit at all times and in all his works to form himself in the life and the works of our Lord Jesus Christ, in everything he does and refrains from and suffers and experiences. And let him think constantly of him as our Lord thought of us.

This penitence is a complete lifting up of the mind away from all things into God, and whatever the works may be in which you have found and still find that you can most perfectly achieve this, do them with no constraint; and if you are impeded in this by any exterior works, whether it be fasting, keeping vigil, reading or whatever else, give it up and do not be afraid that in this you may be forgoing any of your penitence, because God has no regard for what your works are, but for what your love and devotion and intention in the works are.

Our works do not greatly matter to him, but only our intention in all our works, and that we love him alone in all things. For the man is far too greedy who is not satisfied with God. All your works will be rewarded in your God's knowledge of them, and that in them he was your intention; and always be content with that. And the more that your intention is directed wholly and simply toward him, the more truly will all your works atone for all your sins.

And you must also reflect that God was the general redeemer of all the world, and I own him far more gratitude for that than if he had redeemed me alone. So too ought you to be a general redeemer of everything in you that you have spoiled with your sins; and, doing that, put your whole confidence in him, for with your sins you have spoiled everything there is in you: Your heart, your intellect, your body, your soul, your powers, everything about you and in you, all of it is sick and spoiled. So take refuge in him in whom there is nothing lacking, but everything that is good, so that he may be the general redeemer of all your shortcomings both internal and external.

Counsel 17. *How a man should preserve himself in peace, if he does not find himself severely tried as Christ and many saints were; and how he ought to follow God.*

People may become anxious and distressed because the lives of our Lord Jesus Christ and of the saints were so harsh and laborious, and a man may be able to perform little like this and may not feel himself forced to do so. Therefore, when people find themselves unequal to this, they think that they are far away from God, and that they cannot follow him. No one ought to think this. No man ought ever under any circumstances to think himself as away from God, not because of his sins or his weakness or anything else. If it should ever be that your great sins drive you so far off that you cannot think of yourself as being close to God, still think of him as being close to you. For a man does himself great harm in considering that God is far away from him; wherever a man may go, far or near, God never goes far off. He is always close at hand, and even if he cannot remain under your roof, still he goes no further away than outside the door, where he stands.

And it is the same with the labor of following God. Take heed of how you ought to follow him. You ought to know and to have taken heed of what it is that God is requiring most of you; for not everyone is called to come along the same way to God, as Saint Paul says. So if you find that your shortest way does not consist of many external works and great labors or mortifications—which, to look at things simply, are not so very important unless a man is especially called to them by God and has the strength to perform them all without damage to his spiritual life—and if you find that you are not like this, keep quite calm and do not let yourself be too concerned about it.

But you may say: "If this is not so important, why have so many of our forebears, so many saints practiced it?"

But consider: Our Lord gave them this manner of life, and he also gave them the strength to act like that, so that they could follow this way of life, and what they did was very pleasing to him, and it was in so doing that they were to achieve their very best. But God has not made man's salvation depend on any such particular way of life. What is peculiar to one way of life is not found in another; but it is God who has endowed all holy practices with the power of fulfillment, and it is denied to no good way of life. For one good thing is not in opposition to another. And from this people ought to learn that they are doing wrong if they see or hear that some good man is not following their way of life and they decide that what he is doing is useless. If they do not like what he does, immediately they shut their eyes to what is good in what he does and his intention in doing it. That is not right. People should have regard to the true devotion that is to be found in men's practices, and they should not despise what anyone does. It is not possible for everyone to live alike, for all men to follow one single way of life or for one man to adopt what everyone else or what some one other man may be doing.

So let every man keep to his own pious practices, let him mix in it any other practice, accepting into what he does everything that is good and all practices. To change from one to another makes for instability in one's piety and in one's intention. What one such practice could give you, you could also obtain from another, if they are both good and praiseworthy and have only God as their intention; everyone cannot follow one single way. And it is the same with imitating the mortifications of such saints. You may well admire and be pleased by practices you still are not required to imitate.

But now you may say: "Our Lord Jesus Christ always practiced what was the very best, and it is always he whom we should imitate."

That is very true. One ought indeed to imitate our Lord, but still not in everything he did. Our Lord, we are told, fasted for forty days. But no one ought to undertake to imitate this. Many of his works Christ performed with the intention that we should imitate him spiritually, not physically. And so we ought to do our best to be able to imitate him with our reason, for he values our love more than our works. Each of us ought in our own ways to imitate him.

"And how?"

Take good heed: in everything.

"How, and in what way?"

As I have often said: "I esteem a work of the reason far higher than a work of the body."

"And how?"

65

Christ fasted for forty days. Imitate him by considering what you are sure that you are most inclined and ready to do; apply yourself to this and observe yourself closely. It is often more profitable for you to refrain from these things than to go without any food. Similarly, it is sometimes harder for you to suppress one word than to keep completely silent. So it is harder at times for a man to endure one little word of contempt, which really is insignificant, when it would be easy for him to suffer a heavy blow to which he had steeled himself, and it is much harder for him to be alone in a crowd than in the desert, and it is often harder for him to carry out a trifling enterprise than one that people would think much more important. Thus a man in his weakness can very well imitate our Lord, and he need never consider himself far off from him.

Counsel 18. *The way for a man to make proper use of the delicate food and fine clothing and pleasant companions to which his natural disposition inclines him.*

You must not concern yourself about food or clothing, by worrying if they seem too good for you, but train the ground of your being and your disposition to

66

be far above all this; and nothing ought to move your disposition to delight or to love except God alone. It should be far above everything else.

Why?

Because a man's interior life would indeed be deficient if he needed outer garments to guide it for him; it is the interior that should guide the exterior, so far as that is in your power. But if something different comes your way, in the ground of your being you can be content that you are so disposed that even if another time something else should be given to you, you would receive that just as willingly and gladly. And it is the same with food and friends and relatives and everything else that God may give or take away.

And that is why I think it better than everything that a man should abandon himself wholly to God, whatever it may be his will to impose on him, be it contempt or heavy labors or any other kind of suffering, so that he accepts it joyfully and thankfully, and lets himself be guided by God rather than trying to arrange things for himself. So if you will learn gladly from God and follow him, things will be all right for you. With such a disposition one can well accept honors and ease. But if hardships and disgrace come to a man, he must bear it and be glad to bear it. And so people can with every justification and right judgment eat well, if in the same spirit they would be prepared to fast.

And this is probably the reason why God spares his friends many great sorrows; for his immeasurable faithfulness to them could not otherwise suffer it to be so, because so great and so many profits are contained in suffering, and he does not wish, nor would it be fitting, to let them lack such benefits. But he is content when their will is good and just. Were it not so, he would not permit them to escape any suffering because of the innumerable benefits suffering brings.

Therefore, so long as God is well content, be at peace; but if it pleases him that something different should happen with you, still be at peace. For inwardly a man ought to entrust himself so sompletely to God with his whole will that he is not greatly concerned about his way of life or the works he performs. And you ought especially to avoid anything extraordinary, whether in clothing or food or speech—such as indulging in fine talk—or extraordinary gestures, because this leads to nothing. But still you must know that not everything extraordinary is forbidden to you. There are many extraordinary things one has to do at certain times and among certain people, because if a man is extraordinary he must act in various extraordinary ways on many occasions.

A man ought to have formed his inward disposition in our Lord Jesus Christ in all respects, so that people can see in him a reflection of all our Lord's works and of his divine image; and within himself a man ought, so far as he can, to carry out a perfect imitation of all these works. You must work, and he ought to receive. Perform your works with all your devotion and all your intention; let this always be your disposition, and may you in all your works form yourself into him.

Counsel 19. Why God often permits good men, who are genuinely good, to be often hindered in their good works.

Our faithful God often permits his friends to weaken so that any support on which they might depend or rely should be taken from them. For a man who loves God it would be a great joy if he could perform many great deeds, perhaps keeping vigil or fasting or other exercises, and such remarkable, great and difficult matters. To be able to do this is a great joy and a prop and gives hope, and it lends people support and help and confidence in their undertakings. But our Lord's will is to take this away from them, because he wants to be their only support and confidence. And his only reason for doing this is simply his goodness and mercy. God is not moved to perform any deed by anything else than his own goodness. Our deeds do not move him to give us anything or do anything for us. Our Lord wants his friends to forget such false notions, and this is why he takes this support away from them so that he may be their only support. For he wants to endow them richly, and this only out of his generous goodness; and he should be their support and comfort, and they should see and consider themselves as a mere nothing among all God's great gifts. For the more man's spirit, naked and empty, depends upon God and is preserved by him, the deeper is the man established in God, and the more receptive is he to God's finest gifts. For man should build upon God alone.

Counsel 20. *Of the Body of our Lord; how one should often receive it, and with what manner and devotion.*

Whoever would gladly receive the Body of our Lord ought not to wait until he discovers certain emotions or sensations in himself, or until his inwardness and devotion are great; but he ought to make sure that he has the proper will and intention. You should not attach such importance to what you feel; rather, consider important what you love and what you intend.

The man who freely wants and is able to go to our Lord should as the first condition have a conscience free from every reproach of sin. The second condition is that his will be turned to God, that he intends nothing and delights in nothing except in God and what is wholly godly, and that everything should displease him that is unlike God. And it is in this way too that a man should test how far away from God or how close to him he may be, and this will tell him how near or far away from God he is. The third condition is that his love for the blessed sacrament and for our Lord ought to grow in him more and more, and that his reverent awe for it should not decrease because of his frequent receiving; because often what is life for one man is death for another. Therefore you should observe whether your love for God grows and your reverence does not decrease; and then the oftener that you go to the sacrament, the better by far will you be, and the better and more profitable by far will it be for you. So do not let people talk and preach you away from your God; the oftener, the better, and the dearer to God. For it is our Lord's delight to dwell in man and with him.

Now you may say: "Alas, sir, I know how empty and cold and inert I am, and that is why I dare not go to our Lord!"

But what I say is, all the more reason for you to go to your God; for it is in him that you will be warmed and kindled, and in him you will be made holy, to him alone will you be joined and with him alone made one, for you will find that the sacrament possesses, as does nothing else, the grace by which your bodily strength will be united and collected through the wonderful power of our Lord's bodily presence, so that all man's distracted thoughts and intentions are here collected and united, and what was dispersed and debased is here raised up again and its due order restored as it is offered to God. The senses within are so informed by our indwelling God, and weened from the outward distractions of temporal things, and all at once become godly; and as your body is strengthened by his Body it becomes renewed. For we shall be changed into him and wholly united so that what is his becomes ours, and all that is ours becomes his, our heart and his one heart, our body and his one Body. Our senses and our will, our intention, our powers and our members shall be so brought into him that we sense him and become aware of him in every power of our bodies and our souls.

Now you may say: "Alas, sir, I can find nothing better than poverty in myself. How could I dare to go to him?"

Be sure of this, if you want all your poverty to be changed, then go to that abundant treasury of all immeasurable riches, and so you will be rich; for in your heart you should know that he alone is the treasure that can satisfy and fulfill you. So say: "This is why I want to come to you, that your riches may replenish my poverty, that your immeasurable wealth may fill out my emptiness, that your boundless and incomprehensible divinity may make good my so pitiful and decayed humanity."

"Alas, sir, I have committed so many sins that I cannot atone for them!"

Go to him for this, for he has made fitting atonement for all guilt. In him you may well offer up to the heavenly Father an offering worthy enough to atone for all your sins.

"Alas, sir, I should like to utter my praises, but I cannot!"

Go to him, for he only is the thanks the Father will accept and he alone is the immeasurable, truth-revealing, perfect praise of all the divine goodness.

In short, if you want all your sins to be wholly taken from you and to be clothed in virtues and graces, if you want to be led back joyfully to the source and to be guided by every virtue and grace, see to it that you are able to receive that sacrament worthily and often; so you will become one with him and be ennobled through his Body. Yes, in the Body of our Lord the soul is joined so close to God that not even the angels, not the cherubim or seraphim, can find or tell the difference between them. For as the angels approach God they approach the soul, as they approach the soul they approach God. There was never union so close; for the soul is far more closely united with God than are the body and soul that form one man. This union is far closer than if one were to pour a drop of water into a cask of wine; there, we still have water and wine, but here we have such a changing into one that there is no creature who can find the distinction.

Now you may say: "How can this be? I don't feel anything of the kind."

What does that matter? The less that you feel and the more that you believe, the more praiseworthy is your faith, the more regarded, and the more praise will it receive, for a perfect faith is far more in a man than a mere supposing. In God we have true knowledge. In truth, all that we lack is true faith. We may think that what we feel benefits us more than faith, but that is only because we obey external rules. There is no more in the one than in the other. If a man believes constantly, he will receive constantly and possess constantly.

Now you say: "How could I have faith in greater things, when I am not disposed to this, but know myself to be deficient and distracted by many things?"

Well, you ought to be aware of two properties in yourself that our Lord too had in him. He possessed superior and inferior powers, which in their turn performed two works; for his superior powers possessed and enjoyed everlasting blessedness, but at the same time here on earth his inferior powers were engaged in the greatest suffering and strife. Yet this working of the inferior powers did not deter the superior powers from attaining their object. It ought to be so in you; your superior powers should be elevated to God, wholly offered and bound to him. But beyond doubt we ought to consign all our sufferings to the body and the inferior powers and the senses; but the spirit ought with all its might to lift itself up, and then, liberated, sink down into its God. But the sufferings of the senses and of the inferior powers, and the opposition they meet, is not the spirit's concern; for the greater and the more violent the conflict is, the greater and more praiseworthy is the victory and its glory. For the greater the opposition, the more violent the onslaughts of vice, the more does man possess virtue if he conquers, and the dearer he is to God. And therefore, if you wish to receive your God worthily, be sure that your superior powers are directed toward your God and that your will is seeking his will, that you are intending him, and that your trust is based on him.

When a man is so disposed, he never receives the precious Body of our Lord without receiving extraordinary and great graces, and the oftener, the greater profit to him. Yes, a man might receive the Body of our Lord with such devotion and intention that if it were already ordained for him to come into the lowest order of angels, he might by so receiving on that one occasion be raised up into the next rank. Yes, you could receive him with such devotion that you might be seen in the eighth or ninth choir. And therefore, if there were two men alike in their whole lives, and one of them had received the Body of our Lord once more often than the other, through that he could appear like a shining sun in comparison with the other, and could receive a singular union with God.

This receiving and this blessed enjoyment of the Body of our Lord does not consist only in an external enjoyment. Its enjoyment is also spiritual, with a heart that yearns and in a union in devotion. A man may receive it in such faith that he becomes richer in graces than any other man on earth. A man may receive spiritually, whatever he may be, a thousand times and more in a day, whether he be sick or well. But one ought to approach such spiritual communion as the sacrament itself, according to the dictates of good order and with great longing. But even if one does not have the longing, one should incite it and prepare for it and act as it requires, and so one will become holy here in time and blessed there in eternity; for to go after God and to follow him, that is eternity. May the teacher of truth and

77

the lover of chastity and the life of eternity grant us this. Amen.

Counsel 22. *How man should follow God and of a good manner of living.*

A man who wants to establish himself in a new life or a new way of working must go to his God, and with great force and with all devotion he must entreat of him that he will furnish him with what is best of all, with what is dearest and the greatest honor to God, and he must want and intend nothing for himself, but only God's dearest will and nothing else. Whatever God may then send him, let him accept it directly from God himself and let him regard it as the best of all that could come to him, and let him be wholly and utterly at peace in it.

And if later some other manner of living pleases him better, he ought to think: God gave you this manner; and so let it be the best that he could wish. In this he should have faith in God, and he should draw all that is good in other manners of living into this one manner, and accept everything, whatever its nature be, in this and according to this. For whatever good God has performed and endowed one manner with may also be found in all good manners; for one ought to take from one manner of living the good that is common to all of them and not what is peculiar to that one. For a man must always accomplish some one thing; he cannot do everything. It has to be one thing and in that one thing we ought to find everything. Because if a man wanted to do everything, this, that and the other, leaving his own manner of living and taking on another that for the moment pleased him better, in truth that would produce great instability. For a man who has renounced the world and entered a religious order is more likely to achieve perfection than is someone who has left one order to join another, however holy he may have been. That is what changing one's way of life does. Let a man decide on one good way and persist in it, and introduce into it all ways that are good, and let him consider that he has received this way of life from God, and not set off today on one way and then tomorrow on another, and let him never be afraid that in doing this he is missing anything. Because with God one cannot miss anything; as little as God himself can, so little can man miss anything with God. Therefore accept some one thing from God, and into it bring everything that is good.

But if it happens that it cannot be that one thing be reconciled with another, that is a certain sign for you that it is not from God. One good is not in opposition to another; for, as our Lord said: "Every kingdom which is divided in itself must perish" (Lk 11:17); and as he also said: "Who is not with me is against me, and he who does not gather with me scatters" (Mt 12:30). So let this be a certain sign for you; if something good cannot tolerate another good thing, or, it may be, a less good thing, then that is not from God. It ought to bring in and not disperse.

So it was said in a few true words that were added here: "Our faithful God disposes the best of all for every man, of that there is no doubt."

This is certainly true, and he never takes anyone lying down whom he could have found standing upright, for God's goodness intends all things for the very best.

Then I was asked why God did not therefore dispose for men who, he knew, would fall from the grace of baptism to die in childhood before they had reached years of discretion, since he knew that they would fall and not rise again—would not that be the very best for them?

So I said: God is no destroyer of any good thing, but rather he brings it to perfection. God does not destroy nature, he perfects it. And grace too does not destroy nature, but perfects it. If in the beginning God had destroyed nature, it would have suffered violence and injustice; and this God does not do. Man has a free will, with which he may choose good and evil, and God offers death in return for evil deeds, and in return for good deeds he offers life. Man must be free, and the master of all his actions, unimpeded and unconstrained. Grace does not destroy nature, it perfects it. Glory does not destroy grace, it perfects it, for glory is perfected grace. Therefore it is not in God to destroy anything that has being, but rather he is a perfecter of all things. So we should not destroy in ourselves any good thing, however small it may be, even for the sake of something great, but we should rather bring it to the greatest perfection.

Then we talked about one man who was supposed to be beginning a completely new life, and I said something like this: He ought to become a man who seeks for God and finds God in all things, always, everywhere, with everyone, in every way. Doing this, we can always go on growing and increasing, and never come to the end of our increasing.

OTHER BOOKS IN THE SERIES

CREATION AND CHRIST: THE WISDOM OF
HILDEGARD OF BINGEN

TRUE JOY:
THE WISDOM OF FRANCIS AND CLARE

THE LIFE OF THE SOUL:
THE WISDOM OF JULIAN OF NORWICH